GETTING TO KNOW MUHAMMAD

a Rhyming Verse Novel, About the Life and Struggles of the Prophet Muhammad, for Teenagers and Young Adults.

By Walead Quhill

ﷺ - This symbol in Arabic reads 'ṣallallāhu ʿalayhi wa sallam' = 'May Allah bless Muhammad and give him peace'

Copyright© Walead Quhill, 2022

All rights are reserved in accordance with the copyright,

design and patents act 1988

ISBN (Paperback) : 978-1-3999-4238-6

ISBN (Hardcover) : 979-8-3738-6441-1

*I dedicate this book to my child**R**en, nieces and nephews,*
*You're the passion b**E**hind this work, I wrote it especially for you,*
*To learn **A**bout our Prophet and all the struggles he went through.*
*So, get to know Muhamma**D** ﷺ, don't let him be a stranger,*
Pray that one day we'll all be with him in Jannah.

Table of CONTENTS

Introduction	1
The Early Years	4
The Revelation	8
The First Muslims	16
The Public Call to Islam	22
The Backlash	28
Quraysh Persecutes the Slaves	37
Quraysh Plots and Plans	40
The Boycott	43
The Year of Grief	48
The Night Ascension	54
The Hijra	64
On The Road to Medina	70
Battle of Badr	75
Life in Medina	82
The Peace Treaty	86
The Return to Makkah	91
Farewell Sermon	96
The Greatest Calamity	102
The Bracelets of Kisra	111
The Intercession	113
Final Word	119
Glossary	121

In the name of Allah, the Most Beneficent the Most Merciful,
Always start with Allah's name and your blessings will be bountiful.

INTRODUCTION

WHO is the *greatest* human to have ever lived?
WHO had such a *big* heart, teaching people to forgive?
Someone so *generous*, with a **SMILE** he would give,
His name is **MUHAMMAD** ﷺ, that's who he is.

The **BEST** of all of Allah's creation,
    The **FINAL** Messenger sent to all nations.
        BETTER than even the best of angels,
Sent to teach us that all humans are **E=Q=U=A=L**.
A message that is pure and simple,

That there is nothing worthy of worship, *except* **ALLAH.**

A light that will spread near and far,

A guide to show us who we really are.

Muhammad ﷺ the **PRAISED** and **PRAISEWORTHY,**

Sent by Allah to the world as a **MERCY.**

BILLIONS will eventually hear his call,

The **GREATEST** Prophet of them all.

But how can you love someone that you don't really know?

So, get to know Muhammad ﷺ and your feelings **will surely**

                                                                                                     GROW.

This book was made to be fun, so I've given it a ***flow,***

Wipe the dust off the cover and give it a good ***blow.***

If you want to know what happened, keep reading   **B**

                                                                                                                                E

                                                                                                                                L

                                                                                                                                O

                                                                                                                                W,

It all started over *fourteen-hundred years ago.*

Take your time, don't hurry, make sure you read it
S L O W ,

Are you ready?

        Take a deep breath,

                Here we go...

THE EARLY YEARS

To Allah we belong and to Him we will return,
The only thing that will benefit us are the good deeds we have earned,
From the life of the Prophet there are many lessons to be learned.

Muhammad  was an **ARAB** born in **MAKKAH**,
He belonged to the tribe of **QURAYSH**, who protected the **KAABA**.
An orphan, brought up by his uncle Abu Talib, who could neither *read nor write*,
In years to come this orphan boy would bring people out of darkness and into the light.

As a young boy Muhammad ﷺ was a **SHEPHERD** who took care of his herd,

He grew up to be an **HONEST** young man who would never break his word.

RESPECTED and loved by all in Makkah, he earned the title of *al-Ameen*,

The *truthful* and *trustworthy one* is literally what it means.

At the age of twelve, he travelled with his uncle on a trade caravan,

Camels loaded with goods to sell, crossing the desert sands.

On a **LONG** journey to Syria, passing through barren lands,

They came across a Christian monk, who noticed something strange *up high*.

A single **CLOUD**, hovering L
                            O
                                W, in an otherwise clear blue sky,

Shading the young Muhammad ﷺ, as the caravan passed by.

Intrigued, the monk invited Muhammad ﷺ and his uncle in for a meal,

Between Muhammad's ﷺ shoulder blades, was the **sign** of the 'seal'.

The 'seal of prophethood', the **birthmark** the monk was looking for,

"*This boy,*" the monk said to Abu Talib, "*has a bright future for sure.*"

You see, this monk had **knowledge** of the books of old,

He was certain this orphan boy was the **FINAL PROPHET** foretold.

As an adult, Muhammad ﷺ was known for his **HONEST** nature,

He worked for a strong businesswoman by the name of **Khadijah**.

A dignified lady whom he married, may Allah be pleased with her,

They had a special bond of deep **LOVE** and **AFFECTION,**

She was the one who **SUPPORTED** him early on when he suffered rejection.

In later years Muhammad ﷺ would **NEVER** forget,

That **Khadijah** was *always* by his side since the day they met.

When things got tough she **STOOD** firm and never hid,

She **BELIEVED** in Muhammad ﷺ at a time when very few did.

THE REVELATION

Allah, the One and Only, light upon light,
A foundation upon which over a billion unite.

In Makkah they believed in Allah, but worshipped idols too,
Praying to statues made from wood and stone, if only they knew!
Idols are unable to help nor harm them, they are no use to anyone,
Allah is **ONE**, he has no partners, it is Him we trust and rely on.

Even before prophethood, Muhammad ﷺ **NEVER** prayed to an idol,
He knew deep down in his heart that Allah is **ONE**, who has no other rivals.
He was searching for the **TRUTH** and would spend days at a time,
Contemplating in isolation, up high he would climb.

He would find solitude away from the crowds of Makkah, somewhere very far,

Up a mountain,

        he would sit and think,

                in a cave called *Hira*.

One night Muhammad ﷺ, now aged forty, was **ALONE** in the cave up high,

When a **MAN** suddenly appeared, as if he had just D
                                          R
                                          O
                                          P
                                          P
                                          E
                                          D
                            out of the sky.

It was the **Angel Jibrīl**, in the form of a man, sent to the final Prophet,

But of course, Muhammad ﷺ did not yet know it.

Jibrīl, so **STRONG**, embraced him and *SQUEEZED*,

As if he was **LONGing** for Muhammad ﷺ and then ordered him to **READ**.

"I cannot read," Muhammad ﷺ replied, as the angel continued to *SQUEEZE*,

Jibrīl repeated, *"**READ**"*.

HUGGING Muhammad ﷺ so *TIGHTLY,* he could hardly

BREATHe,

Again, Muhammad ﷺ answered, *"I cannot read"*.

With every *SQUEEZE*, Jibrīl's grip **INTENSIFIED**,

And each time Muhammad ﷺ thought he was going to **DIE**.

When Jibrīl asked for the third time, in desperation, Muhammad ﷺ replied,

"What is it that I should read!" he cried.

At once, Jibrīl let go and began to **RECITE**,

The **first** verses of the **Qur'an** were revealed, a book of divine **light**.

Sent down in the **Arabic** language, listen out to how it **rhymes**,

So deeply meaningful,

                so perfectly sublime.

From above the seven Heavens, guidance for the **whole** of humankind,

A book **preserved** till the end of time.

[Read in the name of your Lord who created, created man from a clot – Read! Your Lord is the Most Generous – Who taught by the pen – Taught man that which he knew not.]

(Qur'an, al-'Alāq 96: 1-5)

Muhammad ﷺ, exhausted, felt these words **PIERCE** into him like a dart,

It was as if these words were **ETCHED** into his heart.

Muhammad ﷺ left the cave in terror to flee,

Rushing D
        O
           W
               N the mountain in the cold night breeze.

When he reached the bottom he looked up to see,

Jibrīl filling the horizon in full form and glory.

Muhammad ﷺ was **SHIVERING** and **SHAKING** with **SHOCK**,

On his beloved Khadijah's door he ran to **KNOCK**.

Terrified, Muhammad ﷺ said to his wife repeatedly,

"Cover me! Cover me!

Embrace me! Embrace me!"

Khadijah **HUGGED** and **HELD** him tightly,

SOOTHING and **CALMING** his heart, beating ***RAPIDLY***.

Muhammad ﷺ was worried that his **MIND** might be playing tricks on him,

Knowing the **HONOUR** of Muhammad ﷺ, Khadijah responded with wisdom.

Comforting her husband, Khadijah said reassuringly,

"Allah will never allow this to be.

You maintain family ties and always speak truthfully,

You help the orphans, the poor and the needy.

You are good to your neighbours and serve your guests generously,

And you support those in trouble and who are going through adversity."

How Muhammad ﷺ felt was **TOTALLY** understandable,

His feelings were so **PURE**, so incredibly natural.

Imagine how you'd feel if you saw something so incomprehensible,

Experienced a phenomenon so inexplicable.

It shows you our beloved Prophet's ﷺ total **HONESTY**,

The absence of pretence, his unquestionable **SINCERITY**,

Which only serves to highlight Muhammad's ﷺ **INTEGRITY**.

If this happened to you and I, we would've just fallen **a-p-a-r-t**,

But of course this was no ordinary heart.

A heart **purified** and **strengthened** by none other than Allah,

Muhammad ﷺ is the chosen one, **al-Mustafa**.

Khadijah, **CONCERNED,** took him to see Waraqa her cousin,

A **BLIND** old man and a respected Christian.

Who studied the scriptures and was eager to listen,

He was **AMAZED** by the account that Muhammad ﷺ had just given.

Being familiar with the knowledge of the books of old,

He **REALISED** Muhammad ﷺ was the seal of the Prophets foretold.

Waraqa informed Muhammad ﷺ he was the final Prophet and Messenger,

Such a **HEAVY** responsibility, it was all hard to register.

Waraqa **WARNED** him, *"Your people will call you a liar,*

hurt you and fight you,

I wish I were younger, so that I could defend you,

For there will come a time when your people expel you."

Muhammad ﷺ, surprised, thought, *"How can this possibly be?"*

SURELY my people, my tribe, would **NEVER** allow this to happen to me.

He is **LOVED** and **RESPECTED** by the whole of Makkah you see,

But of course, every Prophet before him faced hardship and difficulty,

The path of truth attracts the **GREATEST** level of hostility.

THE FIRST MUSLIMS

Allah, the Unique, the One and Only,
To whom belongs all praise and glory.

Muhammad ﷺ began to preach the message of **ISLAM**,
The same message taught by Moses, Jesus and Abraham.
The **QUR'AN** was revealed over twenty-three years,
D
E
S
C
E N D I N G gradually, **VERSE**
                           by **VERSE**.

Giving hope in **Heaven** and a warning of **Hell**,
Quenching your soul's thirst like an **infinite** well.
Revelation would come down upon Muhammad ﷺ like the
ringing of a bell,

Sweating uncontrollably, it was hard for the Prophet ﷺ to bare,

Once the inspiration subsided, what was revealed to him he would **share**.

If the **Qur'an** was sent down upon a mountain, it would simply **CruMbLe**,

HEAVY on the Prophet's ﷺ body, yet his heart was so **HUMBLE**.

    Could there be a message that is more **SIMPLE**?

    That Allah is **ONE,** without any partners or equal,

    That there is nothing worthy of worship, **EXCEPT** Allah.

    A message that will eventually spread near and far,

    Now resting on the shoulders of **al-Mustafa**.

Among the first to believe were his wife **Khadijah** and **Abu Bakr**, his closest friend,

The early Muslims were honourable, they didn't just follow trends.

STRONG Companions of the Prophet ﷺ, on whom he could depend,

Supporting and **defending** him, until the very end.

Convinced by the **HONESTY** of Muhammad ﷺ and the truth of Islam,

They knew the words of the Qur'an,

                                   were not the words of a man.

No doubts could creep in, they had strong **belief** and **emān**,

From *The Almighty* to *Muhammad* ﷺ, through the *Angel Jibrīl*.

The impact of the **Qur'an** on their souls was unreal,

Nourishing their hearts like a spiritual meal.

Let's **STOP** and take a minute to talk about the **Qur'an**,

The book that mom and dad have always got in their hands.

Read it carefully and take your **t-i-m-e** to understand,

It will make the hairs on the back of your neck stand.

Why don't you **LISTEN** to the Qur'an and see how you feel?

Its verses give you **gooseBUMPS**, your soul it heals.

It's a protection from the Shayṭān, your heart he wants to **STEAL**,

Don't get it **TWISTED,** thinking the Shayṭān isn't **REAL**.

If he's by your side, you will lose **EVERY** deal,

Making sin look good, he understands mass market appeal.

Whatever's in your heart, from Allah you **CANNOT** conceal,

On the day of judgement, when your deeds are **REVEALED**.

Sincere deeds are heavy on the scales and will act as a shield,

For on that terrifying day, there will be no court of appeal.

So, while you still have time in this life, continually **ASK** for forgiveness,

Otherwise against you, your limbs will be a **WITNESS**.

On the day of judgement when the **BLAZING** sun is above you,

Wouldn't you want Allah's **SHADE** to be upon you?

A day when the **RAGING BEAST**, that is Hellfire, is brought,

And the whole of creation falls on its **KNEES**, distraught.

However, Allah has promised us that His **MERCY** overpowers His **wrath**,

May Allah **GUIDE** us all to the **STRAIGHT** path.

If you **walk** towards Allah, he will **come** to you with sp**ee**d,

These are the **words** of our Prophet ﷺ, what he says is guarant**ee**d.

If your sins are **many**, like the **foam** on the sea,

Remember **NEVER** to lose hope in the **Most Merciful's mercy**.

                                             Y,

                                      K

And if your sins were to **reach** the clouds in the S

Allah will **FORGIVE** them all, no matter how high.

Put your **TRUST** in Allah and he will come to your rescue,

Just **RAISE** your hands and sincerely ask Allah to forgive you,

The doors of **MERCY** are always open...

                    you simply **KNOCK** and walk through.

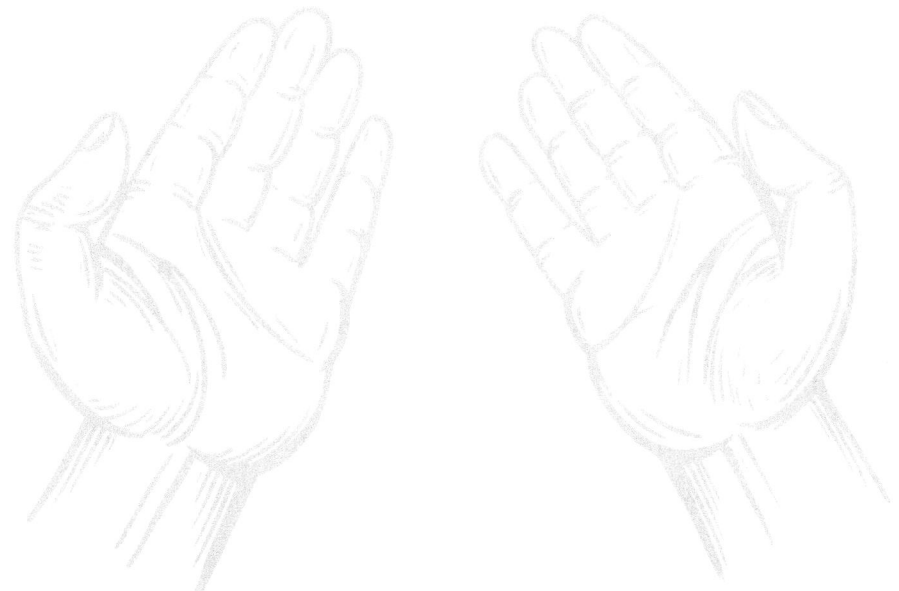

THE PUBLIC CALL TO ISLAM

The word Islam means to surrender and submit,

To the will of your creator, then remain upright and commit.

To Allah and his messenger, our hearts and minds say,

With absolute conviction, "We hear and obey."

From when we are young, till our heads turn grey,

One step at a time, day by day,

Keep making dua and stay focused when you pray.

For three years, Muhammad ﷺ taught the message of Islam privately,

Allah then ordered the Prophet ﷺ to warn the people openly.

To proclaim the **GREATNESS** of Allah and expose the falsehood of idolatry,

On Mount Safa, Muhammad ﷺ **CRIED** out for the tribes of Quraysh to gather.

All the people and the chiefs turned up to see what was the matter,

Everyone knew this respected man wouldn't climb up for any old chatter.

Muhammad ﷺ called out, *"If I were to tell you that on the other side of this mountain,*
Coming to attack you, is an army of horsemen,
Would you all believe me?"

"Of course," the crowd replied, *"Why wouldn't we?"*
"You have never spoken a lie; you are the most trustworthy."

Muhammad ﷺ replied, *"If that is the case then listen to me,*
I am here to warn you of a severe punishment, so take it seriously.
Save yourselves and leave the worship of idols,
Allah is One, He has no partners or rivals."

His uncle Abu Lahab **YELLED** out in front of all the tribes,
"May you perish! Is this what you have called us for?" you could see the anger in his eyes.

In what Muhammad ﷺ had to say, the crowds were immersed,
But after Abu Lahab's rude remark, the crowds started to
d-i-s-p-e-r-s-e.

Abu Lahab's anger overtook him and with a ***FIERCE*** outburst,

In front of all the nobles of Makkah, his own nephew he **CURSED**.

Muhammad ﷺ did not respond, remaining **calm** and undisturbed,

But the All-Hearing **DEFENDED** his Messenger ﷺ with a Qur'anic verse.

Read by millions, in a book preserved,

And in the Hereafter, Abu Lahab will be judged according to what he deserves.

I think now's a good time to **WARN** you about the S
                            H
                            A
                              Y
                            Ṭ
                         Ā
                       N,

Either to yourself or to others, he will try and cause **hARM**,

He will whisper in your ear, when he does stay calm.

He can't force you to do anything, but tries his best to twist your **ARM**,

He will make bad look good, don't fall for his **chARM**.

If something doesn't feel right, your heart will naturally sound the **alARM**,

Say the words that render the Shayṭān **disARMed**.

The protection of Allah from the Shayṭān we s**EE**k,

He's like the lone wolf ready to pick off the **i-s-o-l-a-t-e-d** sh**EE**p.

So, stick with the herd, be wary of his deceit,

Look at how he tricked our father Adam with his deceptive techniques.

He will come at you from every angle, so don't accept def**ea**t,

Of his many tricks, is to make the world seem bl**ea**k.

Shayṭān is patient but ultimately w**ea**k,

Shall I tell you how the Shayṭān can easily be b**ea**t?

Take your time when you're praying, the five daily and rep**ea**t,

Stand before Allah and focus, it's your daily retr**ea**t.

Make sure you do them on time, don't drag your f**EE**t,

Fulfil the five pillars so your base is concrete.

Fast, give charity and if means allow, the Hajj you must complete,

Show kindness to your parents and to all the people you m**EE**t.

E-x-t-e-n-d your arm with a smile, and with salaam you gr**EE**t,

Spend time with your family, quality time is so sw**EE**t.

Choose your friends wisely, be polite when you sp**ea**k,

Who you are is reflected by the company you k**EE**p.

You don't have to save the world but just respectfully tr**ea**t,

Everyone you come into contact with, be honest, don't ch**ea**t.

It's all about manners, this is what our Prophet ﷺ came to t**ea**ch,

He once carried an old lady's luggage in the noon desert h**ea**t.

Always concerned about the poor and the w**ea**k,

For an old person on the bus, would you give up your s**ea**t?

Would you share your food with others when you're sitting to **ea**t?

Do you pick up your litter or leave it lying in the strEEt?

Are you able to remain calm when someone's giving you grief?

Good manners make a Muslim along with strong emān and belief.

THE BACKLASH

Allah is here, Allah is now,
Don't dwell on the past, asking "Why?" and "How?"
Let those chains go, they will only hold you down,
Take lessons from it, don't go into meltdown.
Don't worry about the future, it may never happen,
Focus on the now, be present in the moment.
Life is short, mere seconds ticking away,
Moment after moment, so don't delay.
Allah is here, Allah is now,
Allah will get you through it somehow.

Throughout Makkah, this new message began to take roots and s-p-r-e-a-d,

But **HOSTILITY** and **OPPOSITION**, for the Prophet ﷺ, lay ahead.

The elite of Makkah knew **DeeP** down that Muhammad ﷺ was a Prophet,

FULLY aware the verses of the Qur'an were not the words of a poet,

But their hearts were **CORRUPT**, unable to bring themselves to admit it.

Rejecting the truth and following their **OWN** desires,

They even had the **ARROGANCE** to call Muhammad ﷺ a liar.

It was all about **STATUS** and **POWER**, **MONEY** and **GREED**,

They thought these were the ingredients that would make them succeed.

Opposing Muhammad ﷺ because he upset the status quo,

The leaders of Makkah were clinging on to **POWER** just like the Pharaoh.

The ways of their forefathers, they just couldn't let go,

TRIBALISM was their religion from long ago.

A volatile mix of **PRIDE** and **EGO**,

All the time Iblīs is **LURKING** in the shadows,

Turning people away from the message of Muhammad ﷺ, our **HERO**.

Laughing and mocking Muhammad ﷺ, the elders of Quraysh would say,

"How will our bones be put back together after they have rotted away?"

"Why did Allah not send an angel to help you get the message conveyed?"

"Ask Allah to give you palaces of gold, then to your Lord we will praise."

"In Islam, are we all supposed to be equal, even giving rights to our slaves?"

They feared giving up their idols and losing their trade,

They cared nothing for the truth, it was all about getting **paid**.

Ridiculing and making fun of Muhammad ﷺ, they even called him **names**,
He continued to speak the truth, despite their false claims,
That he was a **soothsayer** or even **insane**.

Muhammad ﷺ was harmed physically, it wasn't just name calling,
Even being **CHOKED** and **STRANGLED** at the Kaaba while he was worshipping.
Abu Bakr came to his rescue and yelled out a famous saying,
"Do you kill a man merely for saying my Lord is Allah?"
The Quraysh wanted to humiliate the Prophet ﷺ and went too far.

Another time when Muhammad ﷺ was **PEACEFULLY** praying,
Animal guts were **THROWN** over him while he was prostrating.
The Quraysh found it funny and were **HOWLING** with laughter,
But Muhammad ﷺ **remained** in prostration until, **Fatimah,** his young daughter,
Came **RUNNING** to wipe the mess off her daddy's shoulder.

One time, Abu Jahl even tried to **CRUSH** the Prophet ﷺ with a boulder,

He was one of the elders of Quraysh who was particularly **SPITEFUL**.

The Prophet ﷺ had such concern for the Quraysh, you'd think they'd be **GRATEFUL**,

But the response of most Makkans was **AGGRESSIVE** and **HATEFUL**.

CAN you believe this all happened to our **BELOVED** Prophet, so **NOBLE**?

Abu Jahl once said, *"We were competing with Muhammad's ﷺ clan until we were nearly equal,*

In order for us to gain status and nobility in front of the people.

Now they proclaim to have a Prophet who receives revelation from the sky,

How can we top that? By Allah, even the truth I will deny."

This mentality of tribalism led the Quraysh to spread **LIE** after **LIE**,

They called the Prophet ﷺ a **sorcerer**, a **poet**, even a **magician**,

They knew he was **NONE** of the above, even by their **OWN** admission.

It's not easy to remain **PATIENT** when people are calling you names,

DIGNIFIED and **COMPOSED** our beloved Prophet ﷺ remained.

He set the tone, he didn't play their silly games,

Muhammad ﷺ **STOOD** firm and was never one to complain.

Our Prophet ﷺ tried to guide them, all he wanted for them was the best,

To save them from Allah's punishment and to advise them this life is a **TEST**.

He didn't ask anything from them, except that they worship Allah **ALONE**,

Instead of giving **POWER** to a statue made from stone.

Our Prophet ﷺ showed **KINDNESS** while he was treated with hostility,

He showed **LOVE** and **COMPASSION** to everyone, even to his enemy.

Sent by the **MOST MERCIFUL** to the world as a **MERCY**,

He is the **BEST** of creation, the most noble man,

Described by his wife as a **WALKING QUR'AN**.

Follow his **SUNNAH** as best as you can,

Get to know him well, become his **GREATEST** fan,

His good character led **EVEN** his enemies to accept Islam.

If someone's being silly or acting like a f**OO**l,

Stay calm, keep your head level, like a cucumber be c**OO**l.

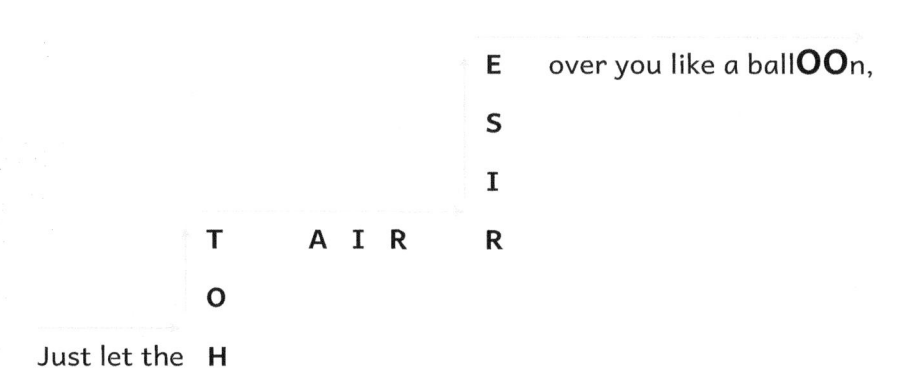

Just let the **HOT AIR RISE** over you like a ball**OO**n,

You've got Muhammad ﷺ as your guide, his face shining brighter than the m**OO**n.

Be patient and respectful, don't let your guard **drOP**,

Shayṭān is always waiting, ready to make you **P O P!**

Be smart, good actions and manners should be your reply,

The way you react will make that person **stOP**, think and ask why?

Should you behave in the same way? Surely that's never the answer,

LISTEN to the words of our beloved Prophet and Messenger ﷺ.

"The truly strong is the one who controls themselves while in anger,"

ALLAH and His **ANGELS** send their blessings upon him.

Whatever he says is **NOT** out of desire or whim,

Inspired by his **LORD**, he speaks with **KNOWLEDGE** and **WISDOM**.

QURAYSH PERSECUTES THE SLAVES

To Allah belongs all the glory,

Let's get back to the story.

The leaders of Quraysh realised that their **TACTICS** were not working,

That their methods of trying to **DISCREDIT** Muhammad ﷺ were failing.

And Islam amongst the Makkans was still **GROWING** and spreading,

So, they focused their attention on the Muslim slaves for simply believing.

Subjecting them to a campaign of **TORTURE** and suffering,

Like **Bilal**, who was **WHIPPED** by his master after converting.

He was made to lie on the **HOT** desert sand, his back burning,

"Reject your faith and praise our idols," his master would say.

However, Bilal refused, *"Allah is one,"* he would cry out without delay,

So, a **HEAVY STONE** was brought and placed on his chest.

"Allah is one, Allah is one," Bilal continued to conf**ESS**,

As he lay in the scorching desert heat distr**ESS**ed.

THIRSTY and **TIRED**, Bilal was in need of a rest,

But his emān was **STRONG**, he did not bow to his master's request.

Yet, all that torturing was done in vain,

Because even though Bilal was in **EXTREME** pain,

And his body was feeling **WEAK** and totally drained,

His belief remained **FIRM** and did not weaken or wane.

Abu Bakr came to his help and set him **FREE** from his chains,

By paying Bilal's master, no matter the price he named.

Bilal stayed **STRONG** and **PATIENT**, he did not despair,

Allah will give him the honour of being the **FIRST** Muslim to make the call to prayer.

And in just a few short years, the Makkans would be looking up to stare,

At Bilal STANDING ON TOP OF THE KA'ABA in the

sun's full glare,

***"There is nothing worthy of worship except Allah,"* he will soon declare.**

QURAYSH PLOTS AND PLANS

To Allah belongs all power, honour and glory,

Allah is always with you, there's no need to worry.

The Quraysh offered the Prophet ﷺ **pOwer**, **wOmen** and **mOney**,
Assuming what they had put on the table was sweeter than **hOney**.
The Prophet ﷺ must have thought that their proposals were funny,
They tried to negotiate with Muhammad ﷺ but to their surprise,
He would not give an **i-n-c-h**, the message was not up for compromise.

The elders of Quraysh were **BUBBLING** with frustration,
Upset that Muhammad ﷺ would not give in to their worldly temptations.
Annoyed, they went to Abu Talib and **DEMANDED** in desperation,
"You are the leader of Banu Hashim, you must silence your nephew,"
"Otherwise, there'll be terrible consequences if Muhammad ﷺ continues!"

Abu Talib was concerned about this brazen **WARNING**,
"This is a burden I cannot bear," he said to his nephew pleading.
The Prophet ﷺ thought that Abu Talib was now withdrawing,
His long-held support for Muhammad ﷺ as well as his protection,
Leaving the Messenger ﷺ to face an even harder situation.
But Muhammad ﷺ showed such **STRENGTH**, **BELIEF** and **CONVICTION**,
Turning to his uncle, he said words to the effect,

"By Allah, if they put the sun in my right hand and the moon in my left,
I will never give up this mission until Allah grants me victory or I die,
This message I will never abandon," with tears in the Prophet's ﷺ eyes.

When Abu Talib heard his nephew's **IMPASSIONED** reply,
He said, *"Go and preach what you please, for by Allah I will never abandon you."*
The next few years were **TOUGH** but to his word Abu Talib remained true,
During the hard times, the uncle that raised him followed through,
Abu Talib would **ALWAYS** be there to protect and defend his dear nephew.

THE BOYCOTT

To Allah belongs all that is in the east and the west,

He knows what is buried deep within your chest,

Put your trust in Allah and let Him take care of the rest.

Islam was further strengthened by the conversion of **Omar** and **Hamza**,

Giving confidence to the Muslims to worship Allah openly in front of the Kaaba.

Seeing this caused the elders of Quraysh to get even more streSSed,

Especially after threatening Abu Talib was of little succeSS.

They've tried everything up until now, even calling Muhammad ﷺ poSSeSSed,

With silencing his meSSage, they were completely obseSSed,

To Muhammad ﷺ and his followers they wanted to cause maximum distre**SS**.

So, they got together and made a cruel plan,
To **BOYCOTT** the Prophet ﷺ and his family's clan.
On all business dealings with them, there would be a total **BAN**,
To put pressure on the Banu Hashim clan to **GIVE UP** their man.
Their food supplies **DWINDL**ED, and their stomachs became **EMPTY**,
Children **CRIED** themselves to sleep because they were **TIRED** and **HUNGRY**.
There was so little food they would eat leaves off the trees,
Or cook animal skin to survive and nourish their bodies.

The Quraysh really put the Prophet ﷺ and his clan to the test,
But Abu Talib would never give up Muhammad ﷺ no matter how hard they pre**SS**ed.

Remember that Allah is always on the side of those who are oppreSSed,

Eventually, after 3 years there was finally progreSS.

The boycott ended and the sanctions were lifted,

But its toll on the bodies of the Banu Hashim clan persisted.

Shortly after **Abu Talib** became ill and paSSed away,

He was like a father to Muhammad ﷺ, defending him till his very last day.

Protecting the Prophet ﷺ and keeping the Quraysh at bay,

A month later his dear wife **Khadijah** also went the same way.

Respected and cherished, **Khadijah**, he would deeply miSS,

It was a marriage full of love and kindneSS, pure bliSS.

She believed in Muhammad ﷺ when no one else did,

Standing by him when his meSSage was mocked and rejected.

Khadijah supported her husband with all her **HEART**,

She was with the Prophet ﷺ from the very **START**.

When there was no one else to lend him a helping hand,

Khadijah was **ALWAYS** there to comfort him and would understand.

Years later he would still feel **DeeP** sorrow at the sound or sight,

Of anything that reminded him of Khadijah, his **love** for her remained **bright**.

In the midst of difficulty, pain or grief,

Allah will provide **EASE** and **RELIEF**.

Our prophet is full of **POSITIVITY, ASPIRATION** and **HOPE**,

Attitudes you need to get through life and cope.

Strengthen your connection with Allah more **DeePly**,

By talking and making dua to Him **FREQUENTLY**.

Because truthfully,

In reality,

The **ONLY** one that can help you is Allah the Almighty.

A le**SS**on that life will teach you constantly,

However, it doesn't mean your struggle has to be one that is lonely.

REACH out to your loved ones, friends and family,

But the first one you should turn to, is the **GRANTER OF SECURITY**.
ALLAH, the **MOST GENEROUS**, who controls all completely,
To whom belongs all **PRAISE** and **GLORY**.

THE YEAR OF GRIEF

Allah has no partners, Allah has no equal,
Allah the All-Seeing, the All-Hearing, the All -Powerful.

With the death of Abu Talib, the Makkans provided no let up or **RELIEF**,

Along with the passing of Khadijah who was now resting in **PEACE**.

This year came to be known as the year of **GRIEF**,

And it wasn't about to get any easier with **Abu Lahab** taking over as **CHIEF**.

Abu Lahab now became the **LEADER** of the Banu Hashim clan,

He was the uncle of the Prophet ﷺ, but he was a **WICKED** man.

At the Messenger ﷺ, he would often **CURSE** and *YELL*,

Always following Muhammad ﷺ around like a bad smell.

He would run up to the people the Prophet ﷺ was preaching to and say,

"I'm his uncle and know him better, this man is a liar so keep away."

Abu Lahab **WITHDREW** the Banu Hashim's protection of the Prophet ﷺ,

Quraysh now thought they could do with Muhammad ﷺ whatever they wanted.

The Prophet ﷺ was feeling **L O N E L Y** and isolated,

But he put his **TRUST** in Allah, and never once doubted,

He remained patient for truly **ALLAH** is the **GREATEST!**

So, the Prophet set off to **Tā'if**, a city not far from Makkah,

HOPEFUL their response to Allah's message would be better,

He met with the leaders and chiefs of the main **TRIBE**,

But immediately the Prophet ﷺ sensed a bad *VIBE*.

They **INSULTED** the Prophet ﷺ and rejected his message to worship Allah **ALONE**,

An angry mob then gathered and **PELTED** him with **STONES**.

The Prophet ﷺ fled the city after being driven out and pursued,

By an abusive crowd, his **BLESSED** blood running down into his shoes.

Worn out and injured in a nearby orchard the Prophet ﷺ took shade, Resting against a wall, he made a **HEARTFELT** duʿāʾ and prayed. Not against the people of **Ṭāʾif**, but about his **OWN** shortcomings he complained,

"O' Allah! I complain to You of my weakness, my scarcity of resources and the humiliation I have been subjected to by the people. O' Most Merciful of those who are merciful. You are the Lord of the weak and my Lord too. To whom do you leave me? To a distant person who receives me with hostility? Or to an enemy to whom you have granted authority over my affair? So long as You are not angry with me, I do not care. Your favour and mercy are of a more expansive relief to me. I seek refuge in the light of Your Face by which all darkness is dispelled and every affair of this world and the next is set right, lest Your anger or Your displeasure descends upon me. I desire Your pleasure and satisfaction until You are pleased. There is no power and no might except by You."

The Heavens *SHOOK* with the Prophet's ﷺ **POWERFUL** prayer,

Allah sent Jibrīl to make Muhammad ﷺ aware.

If he wished, an angel was ready and prepared,

To **COLLAPSE** the mountains surrounding the city,

CRUSHING the people of **Tā'if** completely.

But what was the response of the Prophet ﷺ of **MERCY**,

He didn't demand revenge for the way they'd treated him badly.

Instead, he **PRAYED** that from amongst their children and progeny,

Would come a people who **BELIEVE** in Allah the Almighty,

Associating no partners with Him, the **ONE** and **ONLY**.

You see, this life is a **TEST**, so you'd better not crumble,

You will make mistakes, you may even stumble,

Get **STRAIGHT** back up, don't be arrogant, stay humble.

When things are easy, remember to be **GRATEFUL** and **THANKFUL**,

When life gets tough, being **PATIENT** is most helpful.

This is how we should be, whatever the situation,

Always strive to do better, don't ever become complacent.

Remember, Allah is **CLOSER** to you than your jugular vein,

He knows your **DeePest** thoughts; he feels your pain.

Any problems, **RAISE** your hands to Allah and complain,

The most compassionate, the one who **LOVES** you greatly.

Allah is more **MERCIFUL** than a mother is to her baby,

HOLD on to the **QUR'AN** and the **SUNNAH** tightly.

A guiding **LIGHT**, shining bright,

Like the full moon on a clear, dark night,

If you get lost, the way back is clear and in sight.

Muhammad ﷺ is for us, an **EXAMPLE** and **GUIDE**,

The ***GREATEST*** Prophet, in him we take pride.

Spread **GOODNESS** wherever you go, but make sure,

That in your heart, your intentions remain **PURE**.

Take yourself to account, before you're accounted for,

So that in this life and the next you'll be successful forevermore.

THE NIGHT ASCENSION

By the one in whose hand my soul lies,

To Allah belongs the dominion of the Earth and skies,

We belong and will return to Allah the Most High.

Allah's blessings and signs, the people of Makkah continued to **DENY**,

With Quraysh now thinking they can openly try.

To take care of Muhammad ﷺ however they please,

And the **GRIEF** the Prophet felt in his chest continuing to *SQUEEZE*.

Muhammad ﷺ remained patient despite all the difficulties,

In the Qur'an Allah repeats, "Along with hardship comes ease."

So, the All-Knowing gifted Muhammad ﷺ with a **MIRACULOUS** night,

Full of **WONDER**, pure delight,

To witness the **GREATEST** signs of Allah, such amazing sights.

Honoured by Allah, the **KING** of **KINGS**,

Muhammad ﷺ was taken from **MAKKAH** to **JERUSALEM**

on a heavenly being.

The Burāq, a horse-like animal, pure white with wings,

The root word of its name in Arabic means **LIGHTNING**.

Each **LEAP** of the Burāq would send them both travelling,

As far as the eye could see, so thrilling!

Can you imagine how the Prophet ﷺ must have been feeling?

As he travelled through the star-filled night sky,

Passing through the clouds up high,

Over mountains and rivers below, speeding by.

Until he reached Jerusalem and descends at a blessed place,

At Masjid Al-Aqsa, where the Prophet ﷺ was **GREETED** face to face.

By all the earlier Prophets and Messengers, **TOGETHER** in one space,

A continuous line all teaching the **SAME** message of **tawḥīd**.

That Allah is **ONE**, this is the **ESSENCE** of our creed,

Jibrīl took Muhammad ﷺ by the hand and asked him to **LEAD**,

All the Prophets in prayer with Muhammad ﷺ as their **IMAM**.

To worship Allah **ALONE**, the source of all **PEACE** and **SALAAM**,

Look at how Allah **HONOURED** Muhammad ﷺ the most **NOBLE** man,

Send Allah's **BLESSINGS** upon him as much as you can.

The Prophet ﷺ was then taken up by Allah passing through the Heavens,

With Jibrīl by his side, ascending upwards through a total of **SEVEN**.

At the gate of each Heaven, Muhammad ﷺ was welcomed **JOYFULLY** by an angel,

And exchanged greetings of peace and had conversations so **SPECIAL**,

With many Prophets, as he travelled through each heavenly level.

He met our father **ADAM** in the first Heaven, and in the next one **JESUS**,

In the sixth Heaven he was greeted by none other than **MOSES**.

Inside the seventh Heaven he met **ABRAHAM**, the 'friend of Allah' leaning,

Against the **'FREQUENTED HOUSE'** surrounded by angels worshipping.

It's in the **highest** Heaven, **ABOVE** the earthly Kaaba directly,

Visited by a new batch of **seventy-thousand** angels daily.

Muhammad ﷺ was shown **PARADISE**, with wonders the eyes had never seen previously,

With gardens of pleasure beneath which rivers flow **PEACEFULLY**,

Its soil is sown with seeds of dhikr, so **REMEMBER** Allah abundantly.

The Prophet ﷺ then moved through the **seventh** Heaven, to its **UPPERMOST** boundary,

Where Jibrīl was revealed in his original form and glory.

With **six-hundred** wings spread as far as the eyes can see,

Adorned with feathers dripping with **PEARLS** and **RUBIES**.

At the end of the final Heaven is **Sidrat al-Muntahā**, an enormous lote tree,

Enveloped by **INDESCRIBABLE** colours that are heavenly,

It's at the **END** of all knowledge that is worldly.

EVEN Jibrīl is unable to pass the point of this furthermost extremity,

ALONE Muhammad ﷺ ascended into the presence of the **ONE** and **ONLY**.

NO creation before or after has been **HONOURED** so greatly,

Allah and His Messenger ﷺ, **TRULY** there is no better company,

Where Allah **GIFTED** Muhammad ﷺ with the five prayers daily.

This **EXTRA**ordinary night just kept getting better and better,
With Muhammad ﷺ in the presence of the **DIVINE** being the ultimate pleasure.
The **PRAYER** is like the ascension for the believer,
Through love and devotion in your duʿā's and salah,
You can draw nearer and nearer to the **MOST HIGH, ALLAH**.

We can't begin to comprehend the **VASTNESS** of Allah's creation,
As you look up into the sky and see the stars and constellations.
Think about the planets in orbit, with such delicate precision,
All travelling in the same plane and direction.
A single galaxy has billions of stars, each one in its predestined location,
Taking a hundred-thousand light years just to cross one galaxy, beyond our comprehension,

And the universe has trillions of these galaxies, I know it's too much informat**ion**...

STOP. Try to picture that for a second...

...it's a struggle for the imaginat**ion**,

Of Allah's **POWER** and **MIGHT**, this is all a manifestat**ion**,

Showing the **GREATNESS** of Allah, He is **BEYOND** any limitat**ions**.

And the **SIZE** of each Heaven compared to the next,

Is like that of a **RING** in the desert, now your mind is definitely perplexed.

ALSO, DON'T FORGET...

There's a total of seven H[1]E[2]A[3]V[4]E[5]N[6]S[7] just to put it all into context!

However, you don't have to look so **DeeP** into space,

Admire the beauty in front of you, staring you right in the face.

The natural world all around you, so pretty and perfect,

The mountains, forests and skies **WITHOUT** defect,

The **DIVERSITY** of the plants, animals, birds and insects.

All dependant on each other in a circle of life that's so **COMPLEX**,

And the sea so deep and mysterious, it just demands your **RESPECT**.

It's difficult to understand how some people still reject,

The many signs of Allah, which they continue to neglect.

The universe was not created without reason, pure**LY** random**LY**,

But a design so utter**LY** precise and order**LY**.

Everything Allah has created has been done so purposeful**LY**,

We can only be **HUMBLED** by His creation, designed so flawless**LY**.

Be grateful to Allah's **never-ending** generosi**TY**,

Unable to count the blessings showered upon us so abundant**LY**,

Honest**LY**…

Once you start, the list goes on endless**LY**.

Think about your ears and eyes which allow you to hear and see,
Your liver, the bodies chemical processing facto**RY**.
Your brain, with more connections than there are stars in the Mil**KY** Way gala**XY**,
Allowing you to understand and think about the words you're reading current**LY**.
And what about the trillions of microscopic cells making up the human bo**DY**?
All working together like a well-tuned sympho**NY**.
Smaller still, you have atoms that are extremely ti**NY**,
Made up of protons and electrons that number equal**LY**.
To balance out the + positive + and - negative - ener**GY**,
You see,
Allah has created the world in perfect harmo**NY**.
Yet the beau**TY** of Islam is its pure simplici**TY**,
No **L-O-N-G** equations or difficult theories,
But to **WORSHIP** Allah **ALONE**, the **ONE** and On**LY**,

Because there is **NOTHING** else in this world that is more wortHY,

Of reverence and submission......

      EXCEPT Allah the AlmighTY.

THE HIJRA

Islam is a light, a guiding star,

Hold on to the Qur'an and the Sunnah of the Messenger of Allah.

If you are with Allah, then know Allah is with you,

Remember these words in every struggle you go through.

Back in Makkah, the persecution of the Muslims reached its **LIMIT**,

It was time to leave Makkah, and **DeeP** down the Prophet ﷺ knew it.

He gave permission to his followers to seek protection and **MIGRATE**,

To the city of Medina, in order to break **FREE** from the hate.

It's hard to leave everything behind and start again from scratch,

But to Allah, the Companion's hearts were **FIRMLY** attached,

They had their sights set on Paradise with wonders unmatched.

Still in Makkah, the Prophet ﷺ was now isolated without the protection of his clan,

So, the leaders of Quraysh got together and secretly **PLOTTED** their most evil plan;

To **ASSASSINATE** the Prophet ﷺ, with each tribe volunteering a young man,

To **STRIKE** the Prophet ﷺ with a sword **altogether**, simultaneous**LY**,

In order for the murder of the Prophet ﷺ to be carried out collective**LY**,

So that all the tribes of Quraysh share in the responsibili**TY** equal**LY**.

Jibrīl came down with permission from Allah the Almigh**TY**,

For the Prophet ﷺ to migrate to Medina immediate**LY**,

In order to join the rest of the Muslim communi**TY**.

So the believers could practice Islam in peace and securi**TY**,

Jibrīl also made the Prophet ﷺ aware of Quraysh's misguided audaci**TY**,

In their attempt to kill him with such unprovoked hostili**TY**.

That very same night the assassins laid siege to the Prophet's ﷺ house,

Waiting for the Prophet ﷺ to come out at Fajr so they could **POUNCE**.

Muhammad ﷺ told his young cousin **Ali** to sleep in his bed,

So when they came looking for the Prophet ﷺ they would find Ali instead.

However, the Prophet assured Ali that he was under **ALLAH'S** protection,

And advised Ali to stay behind in order to return Quraysh's possessions.

As they trusted Muhammad ﷺ with their precious valuables **WITHOUT** question,

Quraysh's **TRUSTS** were fulfilled even during this dangerous situation,

Would you expect anything less from the **BEST** of all creation?

The Prophet ﷺ managed to leave his house and **AVOID** any detection,

And immediately with **Abu Bakr** they left Makkah in a southerly direction.

Muhammad ﷺ turned to take one last look at Makkah as he was leaving,

With a **HEAVY** heart he addressed Makkah with such **AFFECTION**, saying,

"I swear by Allah!

You are the best of the lands of Allah,

And you are the most beloved land to Allah,

And had it not been that I was forced to leave you,

I would have never left you."

They left Makkah heading towards a cave where they planned to h**ide**,

With Abu Bakr accompanying the Prophet, always by his s**ide**.

When Quraysh **BURST** into the house and eventually realised,

The Prophet ﷺ had already left and it was only **Ali** ins**IDE**.

"A reward of a hundred camels on each head," to the whole of Makkah they **CRIED**,

*"For anyone who captures them **DEAD** or **ALIVE**."*

The Prophet ﷺ planned to lay low for three nights in a cave up a mountains**IDE**,

Food and news from Makkah, Abu Bakr's family would prov**IDE**,

As Quraysh continued their search for them far and w**IDE**.

Eventually Quraysh reached the mouth of the cave, standing just outs**IDE**,

For the safety of the Prophet ﷺ, Abu Bakr was simply **TERRIFIED**.

If Quraysh were only to look down into the crevice, then most definite**LY**,

They would have seen the Prophet ﷺ and Abu Bakr hiding so plain**LY**.

So the Prophet said to Abu Bakr very gent**LY** and calm**LY**,

"Don't be sad, indeed Allah is with us," with such confidence and certain**TY**.

"What do you think of two, the third of whom is Allah?" he said reassuring**LY**,

To show Abu Bakr that there was no need to wor**RY**,

With the All-Knowing on your side, who controls all complete**LY**.

Then Allah sent down upon their hearts His peace and tranquilli**TY**,

Under the protection of none other than Allah the Almigh**TY**.

The Supreme**LY** Powerful, the Granter of Securi**TY**,

The Everlasting, who has absolute authori**TY**.

Allah the Unique, the One and On**LY**,

To whom belongs all praise and glo**RY**.

ON THE ROAD TO MEDINA

The Quraysh plotted and planned, but Allah is the best of planners, Send your blessings upon the Prophet ﷺ, the greatest of messengers.

When the **SEARCH** for Muhammad ﷺ started to settle down,
It was time for the Prophet ﷺ to continue his journey **OUT** of town.
Abu Bakr provided the Prophet ﷺ with a **RIDE**,
On camels they set out towards Medina with a **GUIDE**.
Avoiding the main route to remain **discreet**,
They travelled across the sands in the *SCORCHING* desert heat,
Taking eight days to reach the outskirts of Medina, which is no mean feat.

Along the way, Abu Bakr was **WORRIED** for the Prophet's ﷺ safety,

He would turn his head and look around constantly.

Trying to **PROTECT** the Prophet ﷺ from all directions,

Riding in **FRONT** and then **BEHIND**, always changing positions,

He had such **CONCERN** for the Prophet ﷺ, along with love and admiration.

All the while, the Prophet ﷺ was at **ease**, reciting verses of the Qur'an **calmly**,

When a **SKILFUL** tracker from Makkah called **Suraqa** caught up with them eventually,

Wanting to **CAPTURE** the Prophet ﷺ so he can claim the hundred-camel bounty.

As Suraqa **GALLOPED** on his horse towards the Messenger ﷺ at speed,

The horse **stUmbLeD** and Suraqa fell off, which he thought was odd indeed,

He tried a second time, then a third, but Suraqa was **UNable** to proceed,

Realising the Prophet ﷺ was **PROTECTED** by Allah, he had to concede.

He then **CRIED** out for forgiveness and asked the Prophet ﷺ for protection,

Which Muhammad ﷺ granted **WITHOUT** hesitation...

...truly he is the **BEST** of creation,

Look at how the tables have **TURNED**, quite a reversal of the situation.

As the Prophet ﷺ was leaving he turned and said to Suraqa,

"How will you be on the day that you put on the bracelets of Kisra[1]?"

Suraqa, **SHOCKED,** replied, *"Kisra, the King of Persia?"*

Suraqa simply could not imagine nor entertain the idea,

---

[1] Khusrow II of Persia transliterated in Arabic as Kisra

Of himself, a **desert Bedouin,** wearing the **golden** bracelets of Kisra.
Who was the King at the time, of a **mighty** empire in Persia,
But keep this story in mind, we'll come back to it later.
Don't skip to the end, be patient and keep it on the back burner,
For now, praise Allah, the **SUSTAINER** and **PROVIDER**.

In Medina, the Muslims were waiting *anxiously* for news of the Prophet ﷺ,
Day after day they would stand at the edge of Medina **EXCITED**.
Finally, in the far distance the Prophet ﷺ and Abu Bakr were **SPOTTED**,
Throughout the streets of Medina, out loud they **CRIED**,
"Allah is the greatest!" so overjoyed the Prophet ﷺ had **SAFELY** arrived.
Crowds gathered to welcome the Messenger ﷺ so **CHEERFULLY**,
With little girls reciting poetry about the Prophet ﷺ so **BEAUTIFULLY**.

This was a **SPECIAL** moment, a new beginning,

Where the Muslims could practise Islam, openly submitting,

To the will of Allah, without **FEAR** or being judged.

Entering Medina, the first words of our **SMILING** Prophet ﷺ so beloved,

Were to advise the people to spread the **SALAAM** amongst each other;

The greeting of **PEACE**, said even to a stranger,

To maintain family ties and to **FEED** those in hunger.

To **PRAY** at **night** while others are **SLEEPING**, so that we may enter,

PEACEFULLY into Heaven, known otherwise as **JANNAH**.

BATTLE OF BADR

Allah has preserved the Qur'an till the end of time,
Listen to it in Arabic, and how beautifully it rhymes.
So deeply meaningful, so perfectly sublime,
Protected by Allah so that we do not go astray.
For over fourteen-hundred years this book has never changed,
Such a miracle, not even a single letter to this day.

The Quraysh were not content to just let the Prophet ﷺ be,

Not satisfied that he had left Makkah the sacred city,

They wanted to put a **STOP** to Islam completely,

All because he preached the **ONENESS** of Allah.

AFRAID that his message would spread afar,

Their hearts were **ATTACHED** to this world, overcome by their desires,

Against the Prophet ﷺ, the Quraysh continued to **CONSPIRE**.

The Muslims would not be left in peace by the Quraysh,

And over the years many **BATTLES** took place.

The most **FAMOUS** of which is the Battle of Badr,

This was an encounter that was like no other.

It was the **FIRST** time the Muslims fought Quraysh face to face,

RAMADHAN is the month in which the battle took place.

Quraysh outnumbered the Muslims three to one,

But the Companions **STOOD** firm and did not run,

And with the **HELP** of Allah the Muslims won.

Supported by over a **THOUSAND** angels,

To **STRENGTHEN** the hearts of those who are faithful,

With the Messenger ﷺ among them, in the **THICK** of the battle.

He was the bravest, the Companions would look to him for **SUPPORT**,

Acting as a shield for the believers during the **FIERCE** battles they fought,

But for the Prophet ﷺ fighting was always a **LAST** resort.

For thirteen years in Makkah, he **PATIENTLY** endured,

PERSECUTION by the Quraysh, for the peaceful message he taught,

But during **ALL** those years of suffering and hardship,

He **NEVER** once took revenge or retaliated.

He was **SPAT** at, **ATTACKED** and even **CHOKED**,

RIDICULED by the Makkans as they made fun and joked.

Can you believe this all happened to the **GREATEST** Prophet ﷺ?

Of **STICKS** and **STONES**, he was a target,

They called him **NAMES**; emotional suffering is always the **HARDEST**.

It's tough to hear these things about the Prophet ﷺ you **LOVE**,

The **BEST** of creation, sent by the **ONE** from above.

We all know what it's like to feel **PAIN**,

Muhammad ﷺ **SUFFERED** the most but his character remained the same.

Easy going and kind, a **GENTLE** soul,

The most **NOBLE** man, such a difficult role.

Year after year he remained **PATIENT** in Makkah,

Knowing this life is but a **JOURNEY** towards the Hereafter.

To Allah the **ALMIGHTY**, our **SUSTAINER** and **CREATOR**,

Please keep on reading till the end of this chapter.

Whatever **PROBLEMS** and trials in life we go through,

REMEMBER the Prophet ﷺ has gone through many struggles just like you.

He was **ORPHANED** so young, his parents he hardly knew,

As an adult he **LOST** his uncle, wife, and many of his children too.

From his message, some of his own family **TURNED** away,

He put his **TRUST** in the Everlasting, all night he would stand and pray.
His legs would **SWELL** with all the remembrance he made,
When he was **ASKED** about this the Prophet ﷺ would say,
"Should I not be a grateful slave?"

He spent many nights without food, his stomach **EMPTY** and hung**ry**,
He could have had **ALL** the riches of this world and lived a life of luxu**ry**.
Instead, he chose to be **HUMBLE** and led a life of simplici**ty**,
Anything he had left over he would give away, **NEVER** gree**dy**.
ALWAYS concerned about the poor and the nee**dy**,
He would spend and give, **WITHOUT** fear of pover**ty**,
Such was the **NATURE** of the Prophet's ﷺ generosi**ty**.

Unlike the Quraysh, who were arrogant and weal**thy**,

To make Muhammad's ﷺ life difficult, they spared no opportuni**ty**.

They tried to **DISCREDIT** him, making things up about him constant**ly**,

They even **DIVORCED** his daughters, an act so coward**ly**.

He was **BOYCOTTED** and **CUT OFF** from the whole of socie**ty**,

DRIVEN OUT and **EXILED** from the ci**ty** he loved so dear**ly**.

There were moments when Muhammad ﷺ felt sad and lone**ly**,

This is only natural, at times we'll all feel this certain**ly**,

Remember Allah is always with you, the **ONE** and On**ly**.

The Prophet ﷺ approached life with such positivi**ty**,

Always **SMILING**, considering it an act of chari**ty**.

If the final hour were to come upon you and me,

And in our hands is a young sapling trEE,

The Prophet ﷺ advised us so very optimistical**ly**,

To plant it, you never know what may become of those dEEds.

No matter how small, get planting those sEEds,

You know how the saying gOes,

"You reap what you sOw."

Then sit back and watch as your gOOd deeds multiply and **GROW**,

Spread **KINDNESS** and gOOdness wherever you gO.

This is the **EXAMPLE** of our Prophet ﷺ, who we all lOve and knOw,

He went through sO much for us sO we should surely shOw,

RESPECT for his **SUNNAH** and try our best to fOllOw,

In his fOOtsteps, so please don't leave it till tOmOrrOw.

Start tOday, start slOw,

There's nO need to be a scarecrOw,

SMILE and fOllOw,

The **EXAMPLE** of Muhammad ﷺ, our herO.

LIFE IN MEDINA

Allah will test us with fear, hunger and poverty,
To see who from among us will behave beautifully patiently.
Allah is always with you, there's no need to worry,
Remember Allah's bounties bestowed upon us so generously,
We ask Allah to shower upon us His blessings and mercy.

In Medina, the religion of Islam spread and **FLOURISHED**,
Tribe after tribe heard the **BEAUTY** of his message,
Embracing Islam, with their **HEARTS** becoming nourished.
They felt and experienced the **TRUTH** of Muhammad ﷺ,
SIMPLY through his beautiful character many people converted,
Others merely by **SEEING** him, immediately accepted.
With a face so **RADIANT**, they knew truly he was a Prophet,

His teachings were **BALANCED** and even-handed.

With **FAIRNESS** and **HONESTY** always being encouraged,

They saw **KINDNESS** and **CHARITY** in society being implemented,

His **MANNERS**, his **SMILE** and how much he was **RESPECTED**.

The Prophet ﷺ would spend periods in reflection and sile**NCE**,

But when he spoke it was always clear and full of guida**NCE**,

Concise and to the point, with an undeniable eloque**NCE**,

Intellige**NCE**,

And

Confide**NCE**.

Always such a positive influe**NCE**,

Reminding us about the very reason for our existe**NCE**.

When speaking he **TURNED** his entire body towards you, facing your direction,

Making sure he's always giving you his **UNDIVIDED** attention.

The Companions would listen with their heads **LOWERED** in respect,

Still and **quiet** as if birds were perched on their heads.

When he ordered them, they would *RACE* to fulfil his command,

They were always by his side; their **LOVE** knew no bounds.

When the Prophet ﷺ would shake hands to give the **SALAAM**,

He would **NEVER** be the first one to withdraw his hand.

Always **GENTLE** and **KIND**, he neither criticised nor frowned,

Flattery, he steered clear of, but gave due **PRAISE** to those around,

Making everyone feel **SPECIAL**, he had a **COMPASSION** so profound.

Giving **EVERY** person such focus and consideration,

Treating everyone **FAIRLY** no matter the situation.

So much so, that those around him would **ALL** feel,

As if they are the **MOST** important to him, his love for them was real.

When entering his home, it was always in a **JOYFUL** manner,

He cleaned his clothes and milked his goat, a man like any other,

His Wives would make mention of his **CHEERFULNESS** and **HUMOUR**.

Never harsh or rude but a **GENTLE** character,

He encouraged the **PLANTING** of trees and **NEVER** wasted water,

Always **SMILING**, **FORGIVING** and **SOFT** in nature.

He would never turn people away if they needed **HELP** or a favour,

A **PEACEFUL** soul, bringing people together.

To worship Allah **ALONE** and to prepare us for the Hereafter,

So, get to **KNOW** Muhammad ﷺ, don't let him be a stranger.

Ask Allah the **MOST HIGH**, the **SUSTAINER** and **CREATOR**,

To allow us to be with Muhammad ﷺ, in the **HIGHEST** level of Jannah,

To be his **FRIEND** in Paradise for eternity and forever.

THE PEACE TREATY

Allah the Absolute, the Lord of the Worlds,
Who sent down the Qur'an, a book preserved,
Read it and give it the time it deserves.

The Prophet ﷺ had a **DREAM** whilst he was in Medina,
That he performed the pilgrimage with his followers at the **KAABA**,
So the Prophet ﷺ and the believers headed out towards **MAKKAH**,
JOYFUL that they would finally be able to perform the **UMRAH**.
PEACEFULLY they marched, but as they got closer,
The Quraysh **SENT** out an army and would not **ALLOW** them to enter.

However, after years of **BATTLE** the Quraysh eventually came to **R**eal**ISE**,

                                                  E.

                                                  S

                                                  I

That **ISLAM** was now very popular and on the   **R**,

Quraysh were worried and thought it would be **WISE**,

To make a **TRUCE** with Muhammad ﷺ because now most of the tribes,

Around Makkah were Muslim and the Quraysh were running out of allies.

After all those years of arrogance and **HATRED**,

The Quraysh were now becoming increasingly

I S O L A T E D.

So they sent delegates to Muhammad ﷺ for a **PEACE TREATY** to be negotiated,

And so, the terms of an agreement were discussed and debated,

FINALLY, a peace treaty was created.

Longing to see the Kaaba again, the Muslims were so **EXCITED**,

However, one of the agreements of the peace treaty stated,

That Makkah this year could **NOT** be visited,

This made the Companions feel **DEFLATED**.

However, the Prophet ﷺ was **PATIENT**, **CALM** and far-sighted,

This was an opportunity for Islam to flourish, he saw the bigger picture.

Creating **PEACE** where once there was bloodshed and danger,

Instead of the tribes all fighting one another,

They would be **UNITED** as one, in a cause that was greater.

The Prophet ﷺ sent **LETTERS** to many world leaders,

Within and **BEYOND** the borders of Arabia.

Calling to **ISLAM** and **INVITING** them to become believers,

Like Heraclius the Eastern Roman Emperor,

To the ruler of Egypt and the King of Persia,

As well as the chiefs of Syria and the King of Abyssinia,

To worship Allah **ALONE**, and to praise their creator,

And to acknowledge that Muhammad ﷺ is the **FINAL** Prophet and Messenger.

    It's not good to **COMPARE** and **CONTRAST**,

    Life's not about who came **FIRST** and who came **LAST**.

    Keep moving on, don't get ***STUCK*** in the past,

    The present is what matters, you know that's a **FACT**.

    Take things **EASY**, don't react so fast,

    Always remain **PATIENT**, **CALM** and **STEADFAST**.

Life is a journey, don't stop walking,

Breathing,

Thinking,

You can't keep standing still...

                      ...you're a traveller you need to keep moving,

Speaking,

Talking,

To Allah the Everlasting,

Who controls everything,

No end, no beginning,

The Most Forgiving,

Ever-living,

All-Encompassing,

The Most Forbearing,

Most-Loving,

How ungrateful we are, but Allah keeps giving,

Allah is The King,

The Ever-Pardoning,

The All-Knowing,

Who sees and hears everything,

Allah wants to forgive you, so never stop asking,

Be mindful of Allah,

           whatever happens, keep praying,

To Allah, the Unique, the One and Only,

To whom belongs all praise and glory.

THE RETURN TO MAKKAH

Allah the All-Powerful, the Unique, the One and Only,
Praise Allah the Most High in times of ease and difficulty.

After two years of peace, calm and stabili**TY**,

The Quraysh knowingly broke the terms of the peace trea**TY**.

They were directly involved in an act of hostili**TY**,

That led to the innocent killing of around twen**TY**.

The Quraysh now knew they were blameworthy and guil**TY**,

Of violating the pact they had agreed upon previous**LY**.

So the Prophet ﷺ gathered a huge ten-thousand strong ar**MY**,

To march towards Makkah, the sacred ci**TY**.

The leader of the Quraysh, Abu Sufyan, could see clear**LY**,

That they could not fight back, the Muslims were too ma**NY**.

But Muhammad ﷺ instructed his ar**MY** not to hurt anybo**DY**,

This day was to be a day of forgiveness and amnes**TY**.

And so, the Muslims entered Makkah with very little resistance, peaceful**LY**,

Which is unique and unheard of in human histo**RY**.

Muhammad ﷺ now had control of Makkah entire**LY**,

However, the Prophet ﷺ did not return like a conqueror triumphant**LY**,

Nor did he ride into the ci**TY** like the victor so proud**LY**,

But rather entered on his camel with his head down in humili**TY**,

To Allah, the Majestic who controls all complete**LY**,

Praising Him, thanking Him and remembering Him abundant**LY**.

For this moment, for this day, for this peaceful victo**RY**,

That Allah had promised and that he'd been waiting for so patient**LY**.

In Makkah, the words of Muhammad ﷺ rang out reassuring**LY**,

"Whoever enters the house of Abu Sufyan is safe,

Whoever enters his own house is safe,

Whoever enters the Sacred Masjid is safe."

The Prophet ﷺ headed straight towards the Kaaba direct**LY**,

Surrounded by idols numbering three-hundred and six**TY**.

"Truth has come, and falsehood has vanished," he said repeated**LY**,

As he pulled down the idols, cleansing the Kaaba from idolat**RY**.

Returning it back to its state of puri**TY**,

The way it was built by Abraham original**LY**.

He then prayed inside the Kaaba, praising Allah abundant**LY**,

At the doors of the Kaaba, he said to the crowds watching eager**LY**,

*"There is no god but Allah, The One and On**LY**,"*

Then Bilal who was once tortured by the Quraysh severe**LY**,

Who was not given any rights nor treated with digni**TY**,

Was now ordered by the Prophet Muhammad ﷺ direct**LY**,

To stand on top of the Kaaba and to make the adhan loud**LY**.

In front of all the crowds, for the whole of Makkah to see,

"**ALLAH IS THE GREATEST,**" could be heard by everybo**DY**.

To show the Makkans that the basis of superiori**TY**,

Is not race, wealth or status, but goodness and pie**TY**,

Just picture the scene, such powerful image**RY**.

Muhammad ﷺ suffered for this Ummah great**LY**,

All the sacrifices he made for us so selfless**LY**.

What was he now going to do after years of Quraysh's hostili**TY**?

The people of Makkah were watching on with anticipation silent**LY**,

Hoping Muhammad ﷺ would not punish them too severe**LY**.

Muhammad ﷺ said to the crowds waiting anxious**LY**,

"There is no blame on you this day, go for you are free."

This was not to be a day of revenge, but a day of mer**CY**,

What an incredib**LY** compassionate manner and quali**TY**.

The Makkans could not believe what they had just heard so clear**LY**,

They were overcome by joy and were extreme**LY** hap**PY**.

They knew only good from Muhammad ﷺ, and he treated them kind**LY**,

By his actions they knew that Muhammad ﷺ was certain**LY**,

The Messenger of Allah, rushing to accept Islam willing**LY**.

Being tested with power is harder than being tested with enmi**TY**,

Because along with huge power, there's a huge responsibili**TY**.

It shows the perfection of his character, his undeniable capaci**TY**,

To bring people together, creating peace and uni**TY**.

Being forgiving and kind, even to his ene**MY**,

This is the lega**CY**

        of Muhammad's ﷺ prophe**CY**.

You see...

This is not a book about someone who is ordina**RY**,

He is the Messenger of Allah, Muhammad ﷺ the praisewort**HY**.

Sent by Allah to the world as a mer**CY**,

An inspiration for the whole of humani**TY**.

A guiding light that shines so bright**LY**,

Such an extraordina**RY**

        personali**TY**,

Send peace and blessings upon him generous**LY**.

FAREWELL SERMON

Be good to your family, neighbours and the society at wide,
Follow the example of Muhammad ﷺ, our teacher and guide,
The best of creation, in him we take pride.

The Prophet ﷺ **RETURNED** to the city of Medina,
With his message now **ESTABLISHED** throughout the lands of Arabia.
That Allah is **ONE**, without any **EQUAL** or **PARTNER**,
He felt his time in this world would not continue for much longer.

So, the following year he made a **FAREWELL** pilgrimage to Makkah,

Many came to accompany the Prophet ﷺ from all over,

To do the **HAJJ** with the Messenger,

Their **BELOVED** leader and teacher.

On the day of **ARAFAH**, he **STOOD** up in front of thousands of believers,

PRAISING Allah, the **SUSTAINER** and **CREATOR**.

The following is what our beloved Prophet ﷺ said next,

It's not word for word but meaning to the effect,

DeeP words with which we should understand and reflect:

"O' people lend me an attentive ear,

For I know not whether I will be amongst you the following year.

Listen carefully and pass on my words to those who aren't here,

Just as you regard the sacredness of this day, this month, this city,

Sacred too, is the life and blood of every Muslim, including their property.

> An Arab is not better than a non-Arab,
> Nor is a non-Arab better than an Arab,
> Except by good actions and piety.
> A white person over a black person has no superiority,
> Nor a black over a white," this is true equality.

The Prophet ﷺ also made mention of **WOMEN** particularly,

That all **WOMEN** should be treated **FAIRLY** and **HONOURABLY**,

Since no society can function properly,

Without **WOMEN** being treated with **RESPECT** and **DIGNITY**.

"Beware of the Shayṭān, for he has lost hope that you will return to idolatry,

But he will keep you busy in small matters that are not worthy,

O' people, there is no Prophet or Messenger that will come after me.

Take heed and be sincere to the words that I say,

I leave behind the Qur'an and my Sunnah; follow these and you will never go astray,

O' Allah be my witness, your message I have conveyed."

Allah then revealed the following Qur'anic verse which says,

> [This day I have perfected your religion for you, completed My favour upon you, and have chosen for you Islam as your religion.]
>
> (Qur'an, al-Mā'idah 5:3)

The Prophet ﷺ stood for **JUSTICE** and **FAIRNESS** in society,

That all people are **E=Q=U=A=L** regardless of ethnicity.

Allah made us into nations and tribes so that we may **KNOW** one another,

Not so that we compare and make fun of each other.

All of us are from Adam, and Adam is from **DUST**,

By the Prophet's ﷺ words you cannot help but be touched,

The **BEST** of creation, whom we all **LOVE** and **TRUST**.

The Prophet's ﷺ aim was to create **PEACE** and **HARMONY**,

For his **COMMUNITY**, his **UMMAH** and the whole of **HUMANITY**.

By bringing people together and building **UNITY**,

Through the belief in **ALLAH** the **ONE** and **ONLY**.

Associating no partners with Him, was his number **ONE** priority,

How can you not love someone with such sincerity?

Who is always striving for us so **SELFLESSLY**,

As he went through *CALAMITY* after *CALAMITY*.

To his Companions he would mention that he misses us **DeeP**ly,

"Those who will believe in me without ever having seen me."

The Prophet ﷺ wishes to **MEET** us, he **LONGS** to **SEE** us,

He sees us as his **BROTHERS** and **SISTERS**.

If we meet him in the next life, we want him to be **PROUD**,

That we stuck to his Sunnah and never followed the **CROWD**.

The Prophet's ﷺ message was **pure** and **simple**,

"Those who are merciful will be shown mercy by the Most Merciful."

Be **KIND** and **GENTLE** to those around you on Earth,

Especially to the one who nearly died giving you **BIRTH**.

So that the **ONE** in Heaven will have **MERCY** on you,

Understand these words, so **POWERFUL** and true.

THE GREATEST CALAMITY

Send your blessings on our Prophet ﷺ, the greatest of messengers,
Sent as a mercy and to perfect good character,
A true Muslim worships Allah and has beautiful manners.

After the farewell pilgrimage the Prophet ﷺ **RETURNED** to Medina,
Soon after Muhammad ﷺ was **STRUCK** by a headache and fever.
He became very **ILL** and suffered with a very high temperature,
And over the days the Prophet's ﷺ body became **WEAK**er and **weak**er.

He became so **SICK** he was unable stand on his own two feet,

The **FEVER** was so strong you could feel the **HEAT**.

His Wives and Companions all became very **WORRIED**,

How would they continue without their dearly **BELOVED?**

Hopeful that the Prophet's ﷺ health would eventually get better,

The Companions gathered in the masjid to pray with their **LEADER**.

What would they do **WITHOUT** their **GUIDE** and **TEACHER**,

But the intensity of his fever grew **greater** and **GREATER**,

As he lay in the **ARMS** of his dear wife **Aisha**.

The Prophets are asked **PERMISSION** for their **SOULS** before they die,

                                                          Y,

                                                          K

                      P and pointed his finger towards the **S**

Muhammad ﷺ looked **U**

He chose the **COMPANIONSHIP** of none other than Allah the **MOST HIGH**,

Muhammad ﷺ **PASSED** away and Aisha let out a loud **CRY**.

In Medina, news of the passing of the Prophet ﷺ spread,
The Companions were in a *DAZE*, it was difficult to accept.
Rushing back, Abu Bakr entered and kissed Muhammad's ﷺ forehead,
As he **WEPT** for the Prophet ﷺ, Abu Bakr said,
"How beautiful and pure you are, both in life and in death."

Abu Bakr then **STOOD** on the Prophet's minbar and spoke,
With a **STRENGTH** and **tranquillity**, he said, and I quote,
"Whoever worships Muhammad ﷺ, then Muhammad ﷺ has died,
but whoever worships Allah, then Allah is alive and shall never die."

He then recited the following Qur'anic verse to clarify,

> [Muhammad ﷺ is no more than a Messenger; and indeed, many Messengers have passed away, before him. If he dies or is killed, will you then turn back on your heels? And he who turns back on his heels, can never harm Allah in the least and Allah shall soon reward those Who are grateful.]
> (Qur'an, Āl ʿImrān 3:144)

Muhammad ﷺ the Prophet of **MERCY** and **LOVE**,
Sent by Allah the **ONE** from above,
Always **SMILING** and **KIND**, a soul so **GENTLE**,
Of **TRUTH** and **JUSTICE**, he is truly a symbol,
For us to follow, such a **GREAT** role model.

The Prophet ﷺ so **LOVING**, **CARING** and **HONOURABLE**,
What he went through for his **UMMAH** was certainly *PAINFUL*,
Enduring trials and difficulties that we would find **UNBEARABLE**,
The **BEST** of creation, the **HABEEB** of Allah, so **NOBLE**.

With feelings like you and I, for he is **HUMAN** not an angel,
But he was able to **CONTROL** his emotions in a way that was natural.
To teach us **PATIENCE** and for us to live by his **EXAMPLE**,
The **LAST** of a long line of Prophets, with a message that is **GLOBAL**.
Despite what he went through, he was so **KIND** and **HELPFUL**,
With **LOVE** for those around him, **COMPASSIONATE** and **THOUGHTFUL**,
Always **POSITIVE** with a **SMILE** so incredible.

The path to **PARADISE** is an UPHILL battle,

While **HELLFIRE** is a slippery SLOPE of sin and evil.

Equip yourself with the **TOOLS** that will help you **DEAL** with life's struggles,

Put your trust in the **ALL-HEARING**, the **ALL-SEEING** and **ALL-POWERFUL**.

Allah the **MOST COMPASSIONATE**, the **MOST LOVING** and **MOST MERCIFUL**,

Stick to the **QUR'AN** and **SUNNAH** and you will stay out of trouble,

A guide to live by, a **COMBInation** that's inseparable.

The Quran is **UNIQUE**, with a theme so clear and understandable,

Full of lessons, with meanings that are **DeePly** spiritual.

Leading us to the **STRAIGHT** path with a message that's so simple,

That Allah is **ONE**, without any **PARTNERS** or **EQUAL**.

It speaks to you **PERSONALLY**, it will forever be **RELATABLE**,

You cannot **REPLICATE** a verse, it's pretty much impossible.

Its style and language are **ARABIC** at its **PINNACLE**,

The word of **ALLAH**, it truly is a **MIRACLE**.

Work hard **I**n this life so that you reach your full potential,

You know deep down that you're extremely capable.

When you put your mind to it anything is po**S**sible,

So that in this **L**ife and the next you will be successful.

Be content with what you h**A**ve, be patient and humble,

Always reme**M**ber Allah and your heart will be tranquil.

Be proud that you are Muslim, living a life that is peaceful,

That we understand our **P**urpose, to worship Allah the Eternal.

Having a soul at **E**ase, calm and settled,

Because be**A**uty is within; it's not all about the external.

But a Muslim should be **C**lean, smart and presentable,

Be emotionally int**E**lligent like our Prophet ﷺ, who of others was mindful,

Giving rights to animals, which back then was certainly unthinkable.

Life's a **S**hort journey, don't take things so personal,

There's no need to be j**U**dgemental,

Or constantly critical.

Leave everything to Allah, an attri**B**ute so special,

But at the same time **M**ake sure you also 'tie your camel'.

Give others the benef**I**t of the doubt, try not to be cynical,

Look in the mirror fir**S**t, this would be more helpful,

Smile and be positive and life will be more beautiful.

Be thankful for what you have, even **I**f it's very little,

For Allah is the Most Gener**O**us and his blessings are bountiful.

Allah the Provider, the All-Wise and Ever-Watchful,

Will put blessi**N**gs in your life and give you more for being grateful.

THE BRACELETS OF KISRA

Allah has no partners, Allah has no equal,
Allah the All-Seeing, the All-Hearing, the All-Powerful.
Allah the Everlasting, who has no beginning and no end,
Beyond our imagination, we cannot even begin to comprehend,
Praise Allah and upon Muhammad ﷺ our blessings we send.

Islam kep**T** growing and spread way beyond Makkah,
It reached fa**R**away places like Iraq and Syria.
Interestingly, many years later,
When Ab**U** Bakr passed away and Omar became the Khalifa,
And the Muslim**S** conquered the distant lands of Persia,
The treasures of tha**T** once mighty empire were sent to Medina.
Within it were the bracelets of the Persian King Kisra,
Which if you rewind and remember,

Were promised by Muhammad ﷺ to a man named Suraqa,
Way back during the time when the Pr**O**phet ﷺ made Hijra.

So, Oma**R** sent for this Bedouin man from the deserts of Arabia,
Who was now old and living in Medina as a Muslim and believer.
Omar placed onto Suraqa the King's bracele**T**s and treasure,
Fulfilling the promise that Mu**H**ammad ﷺ had made to Suraqa
over twent**Y** years earlier.
So **TRUE** are the words of our beloved Prophet and Messenger ﷺ,

Everyone around praised **ALLAH** the **SUSTAINER** and **CREATOR**,
For he has **POWER** over all things, with **NO EQUAL** or **PARTNER**.

We ask Allah to be with Muhammad ﷺ in the **HIGHEST** level of **JANNAH**,
To be in the company of our beloved Prophet ﷺ in Paradise forever,
Everyone say '**Ameeeeeeeeeeeeen**' altogether.

THE INTERCESSION

Allah the Especially Merciful, the Most Kind,
When you put your trust in Allah you will certainly find,
Tranquillity of the heart and peace of mind.

USUALLY, the story ends when someone passes away,
But we believe in the **HEREAFTER** and there's still more to say.
When the **TRUMPET** is *BLOWN* and the **MOUNTAINS** give way,
And the **HOUR** arrives without a second's delay,
And we are **RAISED** up again on **JUDGEMENT DAY**.
Every **SOUL** shall be **silent** and will **obey**,
With Allah's **MIGHT** and **POWER** on full display.

A day when people will be **FLEEING** one another,

Even from their **OWN** mother and father.

When the **BLAZING** sun will be brought above us directly,

With no **SHADE** other than the shade of the **ALMIGHTY**,

Oh Allah, on that day we ask for your **FORGIVENESS** and **MERCY**.

The **WAIT** will be unbearable, who will intercede?

People will **RUSH** to our father Adam and begin to plead,

"Ask Allah the All Powerful for the Judgement to proceed."

But Adam **SENDS** them to Noah, then Abraham and Moses,

EVENTUALLY they end up at the Prophet Jesus,

Who sends them to the only one who can **INTERCEDE** for us,

Muhammad ﷺ the **PRAISED** and **PRAISEWORTHY**,

The **FINAL** Prophet sent by Allah as a **MERCY**,

Everyone will be gathered around him, the **WHOLE** of humanity,

Responding to humankind's request so **WILLINGLY**,

Muhammad ﷺ will say *"It is for me; it is for me."*

Then by Allah's **MERCY**, **GRACE** and **PERMISSION**,

Muhammad ﷺ will go to the **PRAISEWORTHY** station,

Before the **THRONE** of Allah, he will fall down in **PROSTRATION**,

PRAISING Him in a way that Allah has never been praised previously.

"O' Muhammad raise your head and speak", Allah will say directly,

"Ask, and your request will be granted,

Intercede and your intercession will be accepted."

The Prophet ﷺ will say *"My Ummah, my Ummah,"*

Look at the **CONCERN** he has for us even in the Hereafter.

He doesn't ask anything for himself, such a **SELFLESS** manner,

SEND blessings upon our beloved Prophet and Messenger ﷺ,

He will **NOT REST** until our footsteps reach Jannah.

To **EVERY** Prophet Allah has given a **SPECIAL** du'ā' that is guaranteed,

Muhammad ﷺ **SAVED** his for this moment, in **OUR** greatest need.

"My Ummah, my Ummah," our Prophet ﷺ will **CONTINUE** to plead,

For those being punished in Hell for their sins and bad deeds.

So Allah **RELEASES** anyone with emān and who believed,

EVEN if their emān was as small as the weight of a mustard seed.

Yet the Prophet ﷺ **CONTINUES** to praise Allah and intercede,

"My Ummah, my Ummah," he **CONTINUES** to plead.

So Allah **RELEASES** anyone whose heart has a **FRACTION** of faith,

EVEN if it were as **TINY** as an atom's weight.

Those with **ANY** faith have been saved from the Fire it now seems,

But the Prophet ﷺ doesn't stop there, he still **PROSTRATES** and pleads.

He **PRAISES** the Most Merciful and **CONTINUES** to **INTERCEDE**,

By Allah's **MERCY**, those in Hell that simply said **INDEED**.

"There is nothing worthy of worship except Allah," will be **FREED**,

This will be for **EVERYONE**, from the **BEGINNING** till the **END** of time,

Such **CONCERN** for humanity, he doesn't want to leave **ANYONE** behind,

Now you know why, **TRULY**, Muhammad ﷺ is a **MERCY** for the **WHOLE** of humankind.

Muhammad ﷺ the final and greatest Prophet of all,
His Sunnah will catch you so that you do not fall.
I pray that one day w**E** will drink from his heavenly spring,
We will neve**R** feel thirsty again, it will be so satisfying.
The most loving and **C**aring person you can ever imagine,
Inshallah one da**Y**, we will be with him in Heaven.

FINAL WORD

Allah is the First, Allah is the Last,

Whatever you can think of, Allah is not that.

Allah's mercy overpowers his wrath,

May Allah guide us all to the straight path.

So th**A**t young orphan boy, who could neither read nor write,

Became a much-**L**oved Prophet, who conveyed a message so bright.

Guiding people to the straight path, from darkness into **L**ight,

Who came to perfect our manners, **A**lways forgiving and polite.

A simple message that brings to the **H**eart such peace and delight,

That Allah is one, upon which billions of people all around the world unite.

I hope you've gotten to know Muhammad ﷺ a little better,

The **M**ore you learn about him, your love for him grows stronger.

A leader, a preacher, a teacher and father,

There is so m**U**ch more to learn from his beautiful Sīrah.

So always make sure that you strive and endeavour,

To study **H**is life, don't let him be a stranger.

An honest, humble and c**A**ring character,

Always s**M**iling with such a positive **M**anner.

There's no one like him, before or **A**fter him, a man like no other,

To be a Muslim from among Muhamma**D**'s ﷺ Ummah,

Is a great blessing upon us and such a great **F**avour,

The Habeeb of Allah, wh**O** we respect and honour.

w**R**iting this book has given me so much pleasure,

I hope it will count towards my good d**E**eds in the Hereafter.

I pray that one day we'll all be together in Jannah,

In the highest level of Paradise fore**V**er and ever,

Where we will see Allah, surely there is nothing sw**E**eter,

In the company of Muhammad ﷺ, the final P**R**ophet and Messenger.

GLOSSARY

Allah - the common word in Arabic for God

Al-Ameen - the trusted one

Al-Mustafa - the chosen one

Ameen - verily/truly/amen

Adhan - the islamic call to prayer

Banu Hashim - a well known Arab clan within the tribe of the Quraysh which the Prophet Muhammad ﷺ belonged to.

Dhikr - the remembrance of Allah

Dua - a prayer/supplication/request

Emān - faith/belief

Fajr - the dawn prayer

Frequented House - also known as the Baitul Ma'mur. It is located in the seventh Heaven directly above the earthly Kaaba. The heavenly counterpart of the Kaaba.

Habeeb - the most beloved

Hajj - the Muslim pilgrimage to Makkah

Hijra - the migration of the Prophet Muhammad ﷺ from Makkah to Medina

Imam - a person who leads the prayer

Inshallah - if Allah wills, it will happen

Iblīs - leader of the devils

Jannah - heaven/paradise

Jibrīl - the archangel Gabriel

Jinn - spirits inhabiting the earth but unseen by humans, they can assume numerous forms and exercise extraordinary powers.

Kaaba - a cube-shaped building in Makkah, the most sacred pilgrimage site for Muslims.

Khalifa - the leader of the Muslim Ummah

Makkah - a city which is the spiritual centre of Islam. At its heart is the Kaaba.

Masjid - a Muslim place of worship

Masjid Al-Aqsa - the noble sanctuary in Jerusalem - Islam's third holiest site

Minbar - the pulpit in the masjid from where a sermon is delivered

Qur'an - the Islamic sacred book, the word of Allah

Quraysh - a powerful merchant tribe made up of a group of Arab clans that ruled and controlled Makkah and its Kaaba at the time of the Prophet Muhammad ﷺ.

Ramadhan - the month of fasting

Salaam - peace/a greeting of peace

Salah - the act of offering prayers to Allah

Shaytan - the devil (Satan)

Sidrat al-Muntaha - a very large lote/sidr tree whose roots are in the sixth Heaven and it reaches up to the uppermost boundary of the seventh Heaven.

Sīrah - Prophet Muhammad's ﷺ journey through life

Sunnah - the ways/manners of the Prophet Muhammad ﷺ

Tawhid - the oneness of Allah

Ummah - the whole of the Muslim world

Umrah - the minor pilgrimage to Makkah that can be performed at any time of the year

Printed in Great Britain
by Amazon